Text: Didier Poux
Photos: Philippe Poux
Claude Carrier

CATHARE COUNTRY
The Cathare Religion

As de Coeur Collection
Editions APA POUX - Albi

PRINCIPAL DATES OF THE CATHARE PERIOD

1165 Lombers Conference (near Albi) which attempts to reconcile Christians and Cathares.

1167 Cathare Council of St. Félix de Caraman providing for the creation of four Cathare dioceses in Albi, Toulouse, Agen and Carcassonne

1198 Election of Pope Innocent III

1206 Attempt to evangelise Languedoc by St. Dominique

1208 Assassination of the pope's legate, Pierre de Castelnau

1209 Pope Innocent III calls for the beginning of the crusade against the Albigenses. An enormous army is formed grouping together all of the knighthood of Northern France.
22nd July 1209 : Beziers is taken and its inhabitants massacred.
1st August 1209 : the city of Carcassonne falls.
10th November 1209 : Death of Raymond-Roger Trencavel, Viscount of Carcassonne, Beziers and Albi.
Simon de Montfort becomes leader of the Crusade.

1210 Minerve falls and with it, Termes castle.

1211 Cabaret is taken and Lavaur laid siege.

1212 Lauragais, Bas-Quercy, the Albi and Agen regions are conquered.

1213 The battle of Muret, death of King Pierre II of Aragon and crushing defeat of the South.

1215 Submission of Toulouse, exile of Raymond VI and his son to the English court.

1216 Death of Pope Innocent III, election of Honorius III.

1217 Toulouse is reconquered by Raymond VI.

1218 Death of Simon de Montfort during his siege of Toulouse.

1222 Death of Raymond VI of Toulouse. His son, Raymond VII succeeds him. Amaury de Montfort abandons his rights over Languedoc to the French Crown.

1223 Death of Philippe Auguste and of Count Raymond-Roger of Foix.

1226 Excommunication of Raymond VII and Royal Crusade of Louis VIII.

1229 Treaty of Meaux (or Paris) which ratifies the submission of the Count of Toulouse. Council of Toulouse providing for the repression of the Cathare heresy.

1233 Setting up of the Inquisition tribunals.

1240 Rebellion of Viscount Trencavel and the fall of Peyrepertuse castle.

1242 Massacre of Avignonet.

1244 Surrender of Montségur. 200 heretics are burnt.

1249 Death of Count Raymond VII of Toulouse.

1255 Quéribus castle surrenders.

1271 Death of Alphonse de Poitiers and Jeanne of Toulouse, who have no heirs. Languedoc is once and for all annexed to the French Kingdom.

Disc-shaped cross from Fanjeaux - these crosses were numerous in the Cathare period.

The Cassés cross representing Christ as a Bogomile

The Weavers' cross at Mas-Cabardès. There were many Cathares amongst the weavers who traded with the Mediterranean countries.

following page : The cathedral of Albi commenced in 1281, dominating the Berbie Palace and the old bridge over the Tarn.

THE ORIGINS OF THE CATHARE RELIGION

To understand the Cathare religion, we must go far back to its roots, to the beliefs which originated on the banks of the Indus several centuries BC, with the creation of religions termed as "dualist".

Between 660 and 583 BC, the prophet Zoroastre or Zarathoustra, is said to have lived in Iran. His principal contribution was the setting up of various ancient religions transmitted through the doctrine of Mazdeism. This doctrine establishes the existence of two gods, two opposing forces in the universe : Ahriman, the god of Evil or of Darkness and Ahura Mazda, the god of Good or Light. Zarathoustra developed this dualist religion in which Good is finally victorious in its combat against Evil and during the last judgement, men are punished or rewarded for their actions. The influence of Zoroastre's doctrine was considerable amongst all religions which then developed, particularly in Christianity.

From the beginning of our era, various movements of thought developed - such as the Gnostics - who made a synthesis of ancient religions : Zoroastrism and Christianity. It is in this line of thinking that Manicheism appeared, founded by a Persian prophet, Manès, who was born in 216. The latter established a religion whose principles are based on the duality of Good and Evil, of Light and Darkness, and of the Spirit and Matter. In this respect, the beliefs that developed in the first thousand years : that of the Paulicians and the Bogomiles (friends of God) belong to the philosophy of Manès.

Catharism (from the Greek "catharos" : pure) which was itself a neo-Manichian religion spread rapidly in the early 11th century over all of Western Europe and represented a real danger to the Roman Catholic Church.

THE ALBIGENSES OR CATHARES

The terms "Albigense" or "Cathare" were not used at the time by the followers of this religion. They in fact used no special term to define their doctrine. They called themselves "Christians" and used the significant expression "Bons Hommes" to designate their priests. The Catholics derisively called them "parfaits" (perfect). The word "Albigense" was then used by their adversaries in the 13th century to designate the followers of this neo-Manichian religion in the south of France.

The origin of the term remains unexplained, as the heretics were apparently no more numerous in Albi than in the rest of Languedoc. Perhaps we can find an explanation in the cold welcome given to Pope Alberic's legate in 1145 at Albi, which leads us to believe that the Albi people were more virulent than elsewhere. This has historically been proved wrong, however. Or perhaps it was the consequence of the Council of Lombers, near Albi in 1165 - the last attempt at conciliation between Catholics and Cathares.

THE CATHARE RELIGION

This religion is affiliated to the dualistic doctrines which had developed since Antiquity and similarly advocates the two fundamental principles of Good and Evil. The "Bons Hommes" beliefs distinguish the Spirit, the work of God, from the body and all other matter, as the work of Satan. These principles were inherited from the Manichian and Gnostic religions which developed in parallel to Christianity. Cathare doctrine does not entirely reject Christian dogma. Paradoxically, the Cathares identify themselves with primitive Christianity but reject the Old Testament, the sacraments (including marriage) while referring to the New Testament and in particular the Gospel of St. Luke. Advocating total detachment from material possessions considered as the emanation of Evil, the Cathares followed strict ascetic principles. They believed in re-incarnation which brought man progressively to perfection and eternal life. They were vegetarian and were obliged to abstain from carnal pleasures in total indifference to material assets. Only one sacrament was recognised : the consolamentum, through which one became a "Bon Homme" (or priest) and which was granted to the believer on his deathbed. Their religious service was extremely simple and their only prayer was the Paternoster.

In Languedoc, the zone of Cathare influence was mainly situated in a quadrilateral delimited by the cities of Toulouse, Albi, Beziers and Foix.

following page : Toulouse, the "pink city" and the banks of the Garonne.

The crusade against the Albigenses

Throughout the 11th century, the Cathare heresy took root in the Midi-Languedoc region. Firmly implanted in the weaver's corporation which traded with the Mediterranean countries, this religion soon attracted followers in all classes of society, amongst the nobles, the middle-class and craftsmen. The proportion of the population converted to the Cathare religion remained relatively small (approximately 10% altogether). Although the Crusade against the Albigenses provoked a manifestation of solidarity and defence against the invaders, it did not always imply total adhesion of the population to the religion of their heretic lords.

Languedoc before the Crusade

At the beginning of the 13th century and before the crusade swept down upon the Midi-Languedoc leaving ruin and desolation, Languedoc was a prosperous region, trading with all of the large Mediterranean cities. It was dominated by the powerful family of the Toulouse counts, whose domain extended over Haut-Languedoc, Armagnac, the Agen area, Quercy, Rouergue, Venaissin and Viciers counties, Vivarais and Provence. It was a rich influential state whose capital Toulouse was considered as one of the most important cities in Europe after Rome and Venice.

The characteristic of Southern medieval France, which also differentiated it from the North, was the current of liberty and equality which shook the old feudal structures. The best example of this was the emancipation of the cities which elected their own representatives : the "Capitouls". Languedoc society flourished during the 11th and 12th centuries and its culture was spread through the Oc language used by the troubadours in their songs. This current of liberty in association with the lack of centralised power and atmosphere of anticlericalism was to favour the propagation of the heretic Cathare religion. It was within this context

that the Cathare council of St. Felix de Caraman took place in 1167 presided by the Bogomile bishop Nicétas. It provided for the organisation of the four Cathare dioceses of Toulouse, Agen, Albi and Carcassonne.

The Spiritual Crusade

The attempts at evangelisation by St. Bernard and the Council of Lombers in 1165 near Albi were the last efforts to reconcile Cathares and Catholics. They were a total failure. With the election of Pope Innocent III in 1198, the battle against the Cathare heresy took on a new dimension. The new Pope was to employ radical means

Saint Dominique's room at Fanjeaux.

Dominique de Guzman was born in a noble family in Caleruega, a small village South of Burgos. After brilliant theological studies, Dominique became sub-prior of the chapter at Osma cathedral. In 1206, the future Saint Dominique aged about 33, accompanied Bishop Diegue d'Acébès to preach in heretic Languedoc. Adopting the lifestyle of poverty and humility of the "bonshommes", he tirelessly attempted to convert the heretics for 11 years. This mission led to the creation of the Dominican order, also called the "brother preachers".

to eradicate the heretics from Languedoc since they represented a serious danger to the unity of the Catholic church. Unable to launch a war against the "Albigenses", the Pope engaged upon a "spiritual" crusade and sent two Cistercian missionaries, Brothers Guy and Rainier into Midi-Languedoc. The latter was then replaced by the Archdeacon of Maguelonne, Pierre de Castelnau. Despite reinforcement from two prestigious prelates, Diego, Bishop of Osma and Dominique de Guzman, the future Saint Dominique, the campaigns brought little results and the heresy continued to progress.

Aware of his powerlessness, Saint Dominique pronounced the terrible words of malediction : "I have preached for years, crying and begging ... where benediction is useless, punishment will prevail ... the leaders and prelates will gather the power of nations against this region, ruining the towers, destroying the walls and reducing you to servitude."

The Preparation of the Armed Crusade

On the 14th of January 1208, Pope Pierre de Castelnau's legate was assassinated near Saint Gilles du Gard on Count Raymond VI of Toulouse's lands. The count was immediately suspected as he had long been convinced to help the heretics within his domains. His relations with the assassinated legate had also been of a tumultuous nature. Pope Innocent III thus found the ideal pretext to begin an armed crusade against the Albigenses.

He appealed to the King of France, Philippe-Auguste who nevertheless refused to engage upon the crusade, being preoccupied with the rivalry between France and England and little desirous to war with his Languedoc cousin. He nevertheless accepted that his faithful vassals, the Duke of Bourgogne, the Count of Nevers and the Count of St. Pol, take up their arms.

An army considered as the largest in Europe at the time was formed, gathering together all of the Northern knighthood. Placed under the banner of the church, their leader was none other than Pope Arnaud Amaury's legate, the Abbot of Citeaux. Aware of the formidable strength of the army about to sweep down upon the Midi, Count Raymond VI demanded pardon before the Abbot and publicly repented on the 18th of June 1209 at St. Gilles du Gard. Raymond-Roger Trencavel, the Viscount of Albi, Beziers and Carcassonne, hastened to follow his uncle's example. He was too late however and thus compromising the validity of the crusade, he was met with refusal . He travelled to Beziers where he organised the city's defence, then went on to Carcassonne to rally his partisans.

following page : Saint Nazaire cathedral at Béziers, dominating the city and the bridge over the Orb.

The Avignonet crusader

11

The Massacre of Beziers

The crusaders' army descended the Rhone valley arriving before the walls of Beziers on the 21st of July 1209 ready to conduct a long siege. Through the intermediary of their bishop, the city's inhabitants refused to deliver the heretics to the crusaders. Believing they were totally secure behind the ramparts overlooking the Orb, they attempted an exit to scorn the first ranks of the enemy. This was highly imprudent as they were pushed back by the crusaders and in their retreat the enemy soldiers crossed the gates of the city. This was the beginning of the disaster. All of the population was massacred. The chroniclers of the time spoke of 100,000 dead but their number was more reasonably estimated at 20,000. The city was then plundered and burnt. It was on this occasion that Pope Arnaud Amaury pronounced the terrible words : "Kill them all. God will recognise his own." It was indeed an apocryphal phrase which nevertheless reflected the crusaders' state of mind. This event had the desired psychological effect as very rapidly, all of the fortified cities capitulated without resistance.

Carcassonne is taken

Narbonne having opened its gates, the Northern army then presented itself before the city of Carcassonne on the 1st of August, where Raymond Roger Trencavel had taken refuge. The city did not yet possess all of the fortifications we can now see as they were largely built in the second half of the 13th century and in the 14th century. Nevertheless, the assailants were confronted with a formidable fortress, well defended by its inhabitants and its large garrison. The crusaders began their attack from the North and after a gruelling assault, took the outskirts of the city, thus entirely depriving the inhabitants of their water supply. Exhausted by the battle and suffering from lack of water and dysentery, they were to meet with no pity from the crusaders who rejected the attempt at reconciliation by King Pierre II of Aragon. The young viscount Raymond Roger Trencavel ventured into the enemy camp to negotiate a surrender. Against all expectations and in violation of the principles of chivalry, he was taken prisoner by the Catholic army. Deprived of their lord, the inhabitants opened the gates of the city, or according to another version, fled by way of the underground passages.

Within a few weeks, the viscounty of Beziers and Carcassonne, one of the most prestigious seigniories of Languedoc, fell into the crusaders' hands in the face of their powerless suzerains - the Count of Toulouse and the King of Aragon. The unfortunate viscount of Trencavel died in mysterious conditions on the 10th of November 1209, a prisoner in his own castle.

Given the lack of enthusiasm of the Northern lords who were reluctant to compromise themselves in despoiling the Southern territories, Pope Arnaud-Amaury's legate gave the conquered viscounty to Simon de Montfort. The latter was a small lord from Ile de France who had distinguished himself during the battles. The Church could not have found a better supporter than this cruel and ambitious warrior who for nine years led the crusaders in a tireless struggle against the Midi-Languedoc.

Carcassonne : Aude door, Justice tower and counts castle.

14

The war of the castles

Many of the Northern lords returned to their lands once their crusade service was terminated. After the initial terror which had struck the South, the inhabitants of this region began to organise their defence and numerous fortresses considered impregnable prepared their resistance. Simon de Montfort and the crusade army began a long period of conquest, of cruel and pitiless battles and sieges which finally resulted in neither conquerors nor conquered. We will only mention here the most striking events as the chapter concerning the castles will give more detailed facts.

Having in vain attempted to take Cabaret Castle in February 1210, Simon de Montfort laid siege to the town of Minerve. After six weeks of resistance, the inhabitants, deprived of water, were forced to surrender. The garrison was spared but one hundred and fifty heretics who refused to renounce their faith were burned alive. Termes Castle, a formidable fortress was only taken after a four-month effort by the crusaders whose victory was due largely to the ravages of dysentery amongst the castle's occupants. After the fall of Cabaret and content with his victories, Simon de Montfort began the siege of Lavaur in March 1211. Reputed for its community of

The dove of Minerve, sculpted in stone by J.L. Séverac in memory of the 150 Cathares burnt at the stake.

Simon de Montfort

Simon, Lord of Montfort and Espéron, Count of Leicester in England. Aged about 50 in 1209, tall, elegant and good-looking he was in the prime of life. Having proved his military worth in the Holy Land, he was the "glaive of the Church" for 9 years in the Midi region. Considered fanatically pious, cruel and ambitious, this small lord from Ile de France became the key figure of the crusade.

Saint Alain cathedral of Lavaur.

treal, the first of many to be hanged, he and his eighty knights then had their throats slit. As for Dame Guiraude, the "Song of Roland" tells us that "she was thrown into a well. She was buried under the stones to the great agitation of the townspeople ... for she was good and charitable." Lavaur holds the unfortunate record of the largest number of persons burnt at the stake. Four hundred heretics, singing as they went, were led to the flames to be burnt alive.

The covered market square in Cordes.

Founded in 1222 by Count Raymond VII of Toulouse, Cordes was granted numerous franchises and was exempted from various taxes in order to attract the poorer people of the region and develop a new centre of resistance. Until the beginning of the 14th century, Cordes remained a large gathering place for heretics and there are many tales recounting the fate of inquisitors thrown into the well on the marketplace.

Cathares protected by Guiraude de Lavaur, herself a heretic, the town courageously resisted the attack. On the 3rd of May, an opening was made in the town wall and the crusaders succeeded in entering. The reprisals were terrible. The gallows having broken with the weight of Aimery de Mon-

The battles of Castelnaudary and Muret

It was now evident that the crusade against the Albigenses was becoming a war of conquest. Count Raymond VI of Toulouse and Roger Bernard, the Count of Foix, united to fight the invaders. After his failure before the walls of Toulouse, Simon de Montfort had to confront for the first time, a unified army of Southern lords at Castelnaudary in September 1211. After a bloody battle whose outcome was uncertain, both camps claimed victory. However the territorial ambitions of Simon de Montfort, nicknamed the "Crusade Lion", began to worry the King of France, the Pope and especially the King of Aragon. The latter feared that his claims over Languedoc would be seriously menaced. In September 1213, Pierre II of Aragon's army, basking in the glory of its recent victory over the Moors at Las Navas de Tolosa, united with that of the Count of Toulouse. They laid siege to Muret Castle which Simon de Montfort had just captured. The ensuing battle which took place on the 12th of September 1213 seemed to favour the victorious outcome of the South who outnumbered the enemy ten to one. Simon de Montfort's military skill was however not taken into account and he was able to transform this epic combat into a crushing victory for the crusaders. In the confusion of the battle, the King of Aragon was killed, amplifying the rout of the southerners who were massacred. The Count of Toulouse took refuge in the capital and Simon de Montfort's triumph was total, thus reinforcing his image of invincibility. The consequences of this defeat were disastrous : the entire South capitulated and in June 1215, the crusaders entered Toulouse and Raymond VI and his young son fled to the English court.

Saint Michel collegial at Castelnaudary.

The death of Simon de Montfort

Pope Innocent III, the principal protagonist and supporter of the crusade, died on the 16th of July 1216. Taking advantage of this event full of consequences, the young Raymond VII of Toulouse landed in Marseille with the intention of reconquering his domains. After a victory at Beaucaire and accompanied by his father, he entered Toulouse on the 13th of September 1217, the French knights having already been expelled by the inhabitants. Humiliated and defeated, Simon de Montfort immediately began a siege of the city which was to last for months. On the 25th of June 1218, a stone thrown by a catapult manoeuvred, ac-

La Pierre du Siège (13th century), a low relief conserved inside Saint Nazaire basilica at Carcassonne. It could well represent the siège of Toulouse in 1218 and the death of Simon de Montfort

Saint Sernin basilica at Toulouse, a masterpiece of Languedoc Romanesque art.

cording to an anecdote, by the women of Toulouse, hit the "Crusade Lion" mortally wounding him on the head. His grim prophesy was thus fulfilled - "Either this city will kill me or I will kill it." With the death of Simon de Montfort, a wave of relief swept over the entire Midi-Languedoc.

Simon's son, Amaury de Montfort then raised the siege of Toulouse and despite the support of Louis VIII, the son of King Philippe Auguste, he was beaten at Bazièges and Castelnaudary. In 1222, he abandoned all of his rights over Languedoc to the French Crown. The Count of Toulouse, Raymond VI, Roger Bernard of Foix and the King of France, Philippe Auguste were to die within short intervals of each other.

The Royal Crusade and the Treaty of Meaux

On the 15th of January 1224, Amaury de Montfort finally left Carcassonne and the Languedoc region took on a relatively peaceful aspect. The dispossessed lords returned to their castles, amongst them the young Raymond Trencavel who recovered his viscounty. The Cathares were able to take a second breath.

The King of France Philippe Auguste had never wished to be involved with the crusade but this time, the occasion was extremely favourable for his son, Louis VIII to bring the Southern lands into the fold of the Crown. In December 1225 at the Council of Bourges, the Count of Toulouse was declared enemy of the Church and the King of France. Strongly encouraged by Pope Honorius III and by his ambitious wife, Blanche de Castille, Louis VIII began a new crusade in May 1226. Descending through the Rhone valley, the Royal army laid siege to the city of Avignon which valiantly resisted. However, at the same time, all of the large Southern towns surrendered, and when Avignon finally did so in turn, the Royal crusade was practically terminated. Toulouse nevertheless resisted and the King, who was sick, had to resign himself to returning to France. He was never to arrive as he died on the way at Montpensier in Auvergne. The viscounty of Beziers, Carcassonne and Albi having been annexed, the only remaining problem was that of Toulouse. It was diplomatically solved by Blanche de Castille, acting in the name of her son Louis IX (the future Saint Louis) and the Pope's legate, Romain de Saint Ange.

The conditions imposed upon the young Count of Toulouse, Raymond VII during the Treaty of Meaux in 1229 were draconian and humiliating. They provided in particular for the reduction of his domains by two thirds and above all, the marriage of his only daughter to Louis IX's brother, Alphonse de Poitiers. In other words on the death of Raymond VII, the county of Toulouse would be annexed to the Kingdom of France.

The Inquisition

Following the Treaty of Meaux which provided for the total eradication of the Cathares, the Council of Toulouse presided by Romain de Saint Ange set up the Inquisition procedures. This institution was to be used for centuries all over Christendom. The Inquisition Tribunals were composed of Dominican brothers, an order created by Saint Dominique, and were answerable for their actions only before the Pope. Due to their absolute power, the repression in the Midi-Languedoc was terrifying and pitiless and the Inquisition prisons were soon full.

The last attempts at resistance

As the entire Midi was conquered and the Cathares pursued, resistance was organised at the borders of Languedoc and Aragon. The formidable castles of Fenouillèdes, Quéribus, Peyrepertuse and Puilaurens were fortified constructions on rocky spurs. Together with the impregnable fortress of Montségur, they became refuges for the fleeing Cathares. For years, thousands of pilgrims came to listen to the sermons of the "perfects" who themselves often left their hideouts to preach in the surrounding countryside. The most famous of them was Guilhabert de Castres who eluded the Inquisitors many times to administer the consolamentum sacrament to the dying.

During the summer of 1240, an army of dispossessed lords, commanded by Raymond Trencavel, also dispossessed and reinforced by a battalion from Aragon, tried to reconquer their domains. After a gruelling siege at Carcassonne, the Southerners were pushed back towards Aragon by the Royal army who took Peyrepertuse castle at the same time.

The castle of the Counts of Foix, perched on its rocky spur, resisted during the entire crusade, then surrendered during an expedition sent by the King of France Philippe le Hardi, in 1272.

The massacre of Avignonet

The pitiless repression of the Inquisition tribunals continued and heretics were burnt at the stake all over the country. A detachment of knights was sent from Montségur to Avignonet in the Lauragais region where they massacred the Inquisitors and their assistants. This event provoked a wave of insurrection in the Midi, led by Count Raymond VII, who was indeed implicated in the Avignonet affair. The revolt was rapidly brought under control by St Louis and Raymond VII was forced to demand pardon before the King of France and the Church. The Inquisition was not to forget the insult and Montségur, considered as "the synagogue of heresy" was to live its last hours of independence.

The massacre of the inquisitors at Avignonet.

The capture of Montségur

"The dragon's head must be chopped off" - These were Blanche de Castille's words in May 1243 when the Royal army of eight thousand men arrived at the foot of Montségur citadel. On its rocky spur or "pog" at 1207 metres altitude, the fortress commanded by Pierre Roger de Mirepoix seemed practically impregnable. During the winter however, Basque mountain people climbed the cliff and set up a catapult on the eastern ridge. From eighty metres away, they were to bombard the ramparts of the castle with boulders. In March 1244, the fortress surrendered on condition that its soldiers were spared. On the 16th of March, more than two hundred heretics refusing to renounce their faith, were thrown into an enormous fire at "prat des cramats" at the foot of the site. With the fall of Montségur which was the symbol of Cathare resistance, the hopes of the entire Languedoc people were dashed.

Quéribus and Puilaurens castles surrendered in 1255, creating a new border between the French Kingdom and Aragon, then Spain.

The Count of Toulouse died in 1249 without a male heir. In 1271, when Alphonse de Poitiers and Jeanne de Toulouse also died, Languedoc became part of the French Crown.

The last known Cathare, Guillaume Bélibaste was burned alive in 1321 at Villerouge-Thermenès.

Stele erected in memory of the Cathares who perished at the stake at Montségur (Als catars, Als martirs del pur amor crestians 16th March 1244)

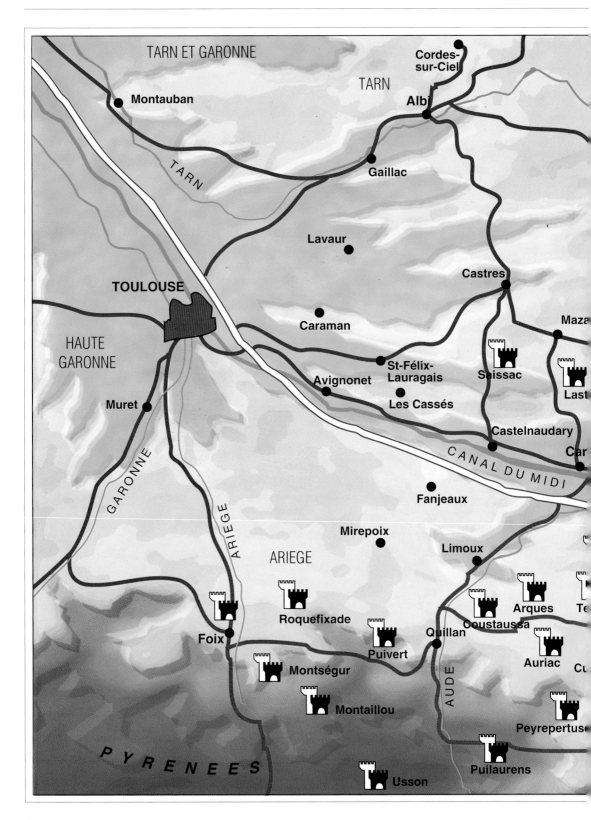

TARN ET GARONNE

Cordes-sur-Ciel

TARN

Montauban

Albi

TARN

Gaillac

Lavaur

Castres

TOULOUSE

Maza

HAUTE
GARONNE

Caraman

Saissac

Last

St-Félix-Lauragais

Avignonet

GARONNE

Muret

Les Cassés

Castelnaudary

Car

CANAL DU MIDI

ARIEGE

Fanjeaux

Mirepoix

Limoux

ARIEGE

Roquefixade

Arques

Te

Coustaussa

Foix

Puivert

Quillan

Auriac

Cu

Montségur

AUDE

Montaillou

Peyrepertus

Puilaurens

PYRENEES

Usson

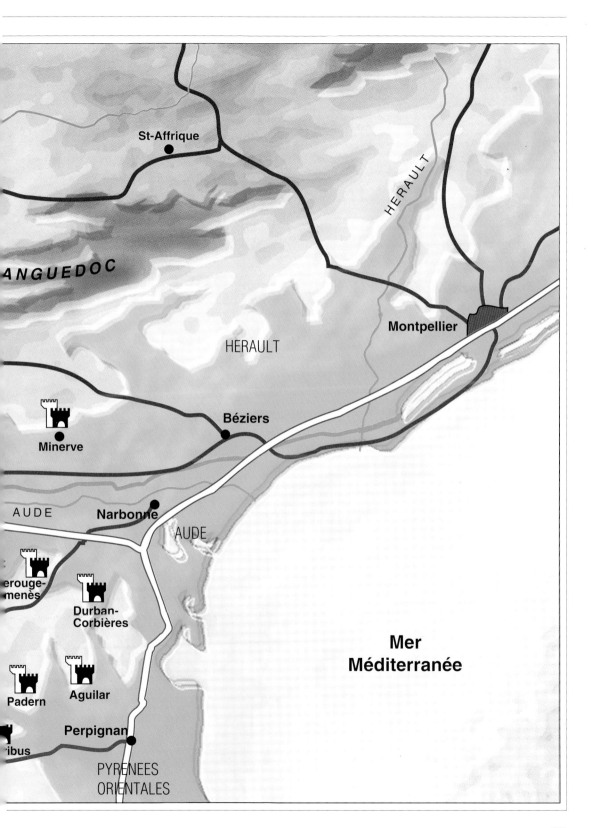

St-Affrique

HERAULT

LANGUEDOC

HERAULT

Montpellier

Minerve

Béziers

AUDE

Narbonne

AUDE

erouge-
menès

Durban-
Corbières

Padern

Aguilar

Perpignan

ibus

PYRENEES
ORIENTALES

Mer
Méditerranée

The four castles of Lastours on their rocky spur.

LASTOURS

Situated between Conques-sur-Orbiel and Mas Cabardès, overlooking the Orbiel and Grésilhou valleys, are the four castles of Lastours : Cabaret, Tour Régine, Fleur-Espine and Querthineux. It is an impressive defence body whose walls blend in with the stones of the rocky spurs on which it is built.

A path leads up to the four citadels, harmoniously framed by the tall silhouettes of cypress trees. The first castle, Cabaret, already mentioned in 1063, is characterised by its square dungeon, its main body and a wall which still conserves its crenelations.

Tour Régine (or Royal tower) was undoubtedly built after the crusade. Of smaller

From cabaret Castle, a view over Tour Régine and Querthineux.

Lastours - Cabaret Castle.

dimensions it is composed of a circular tower protected by a wall.

Fleur-Espine (formerly called Surdespine) is the most dilapidated and overlooks the other castles.

Querthineux, situated further down features a large cylindrical dungeon joined onto a massive wall. The numerous caves beneath the castles have sustained the legend according to which the inhabitants of Carcassonne during the capture of the city in 1209, fled by way of the underground passages to the Lastours fortresses.

During the crusade, Simon de Montfort vainly attempted to capture Lastours which sheltered a large community of Cathares protected by Lord Pierre Roger de Cabaret. High up from his hideout, Pierre Roger harassed the rear lines of Simon de Montfort's army. Finally infuriated, the latter thought up a macabre plan to discourage his enemy. Following the capture of Bram, he chose about a hundred men amongst the prisoners and cut off their ears, lips and noses and gouged out their eyes. One of them was spared an eye in order to lead his unfortunate companions in a bloody cohort to the ramparts of Lastours. This tragic episode did not break the determination of Pierre Roger de Cabaret, who was nevertheless forced to negotiate a surrender after the fall of Termes castle.

Lastours - Fleur-Espine Castle.

Aerial view of the town of Minerve.

Saissac Castle

MINERVE

In an exceptional site, surrounded by arid countryside, Minerve is built on a rocky spur overlooking deep gorges. Situated at the confluent of the Briant and Cesse rivers, which have formed two natural bridges in the limestone rock face, the small medieval town nestles inside its old walls. Around St. Etienne church built in the 12th and 13th centuries, we can discover the old streets, fortified doors, posterns and the castle ruins.

In June 1210, Simon de Montfort encouraged by the Narbonne inhabitants who did not seem particularly fond of their Minerve neighbours, began the siege of the town. The fortress was strong and the garrison commanded by Viscount Guillaume de Minerve, resisted the enemy assaults. The attackers set up four catapults which bombarded the town ramparts. One of them destroyed the covered well descending to the stream thus depriving the inhabitants of drinking water in the hot month of August. After a siege of six weeks, Guillaume de Minerve was forced to surrender. The garrison was not taken prisoner and the heretics who would renounce their faith were also promised freedom. Before the protests of certain knights, the legate Armand Amaury replied : "Have no fear, very few will convert." He was right as none of them did so and one hundred and fifty men and women threw themselves into the flames.

SAISSAC

North of Carcassonne in the "Montagne Noire" area, Saissac castle which once sheltered a Cathare community, was the property of Bertrand de Saissac, the young viscount Trencavel's guardian. The castle ruins below the village date from after the crusade. In the village which features medieval houses, we can see two 12th century towers which are said to be vestiges of the former castle.

MONTSEGUR

Situated in Ariège, South of Lavelanet, Montségur was one of the last pockets of resistance in Languedoc during the crusade against the Albigenses. Suspended between sky and earth on its rocky spur, also called "pog" in dialect, the fortress was built at an altitude of 1207 metres and still conserves its aura of prestige and mystery.

Both a sanctuary and a fortress it is the only one really built by the Cathares. Montségur bequeaths us its great moments of glory and tragedy during the Albigense epic. Its exceptional site, the legends surrounding it and the symbol of the Cathare religion that it continues to perpetrate endow it with such a power of attraction that the visitor cannot remain indifferent before this aerial citadel.

Montségur - "sure" or "safe mountain" -

Montségur castle, situated on its rocky spur at 1207 metres altitude, was considered as the "synagogue of Satan".

had always been occupied by man. In the early 13th century, the Cathares decided to make it their refuge and the lord of the area, Raymond de Péreille, built the first fortifications in 1204. During the entire crusade, the citadel which had not been constructed for military reasons, was to serve as a refuge and place of pilgrimage for the Cathares and their sympathisers. A large community of heretics, estimated at 500, settled at Montségur and the great Cathare bishop, Guilhabert de Castres took refuge here. During the long years of repression, Montségur exercised a great influence over all of Languedoc. In 1241, on the request of the King of France, Raymond VII of Toulouse attempted an initial siege, but lacking conviction, failed to accomplish it successfully. After the massacre of the Inquisitors at Avignonet in 1242, lead by the knights from Montségur, the destiny of "the synagogue of Satan", a Catholic term, seemed decided upon.

The siege begun by the crusaders' army in May 1243 was to last ten months. The garrison commanded by Pierre Roger de Mirepoix resisted valiantly, however the assailants set up a catapult on the eastern ridge and riddled the castle walls. Helped by treachery, they were able to reach the summit and took over the barbican, the castle's essential defensive element. On the 1st of March 1244, Raymond de Péreille and Pierre Roger de Mirepoix began negotiations for the castle's surrender. A stele is situated at the "prat des cramats", the field where the martyrs were burnt. It now commemorates the death of 200 heretics who, refusing to give up their faith, perished in an enormous fire built at the foot of the castle.

Montségur was given to Guy de Lévis, the faithful companion of Simon de Montfort. Since it was of little strategic interest, the citadel was abandoned in the 16th century.

Numerous legends and speculations have sprung up around the site of Montségur. Some such as the German Otto Rahn and the Nazis during the second world war have said it contained the Holy Grail. Others, such as Fernand Niel have put forward the hypothesis of a solar temple, thus supporting the theory that the Cathares were sunworshippers.

Nowadays, the mystery which has still found no explanation remains. During the siege of Montségur and according to witnesses, in the winter of 1243, two men - Pierre Bonnet, deacon of Toulouse and Mathieu, left the castle carrying the treasure with them. Later, during the surrender, four other men succeeded in escaping. What was their mission ? Did they join the first two to help them carry off the treasure ? Did the treasure really exist and if so, what was its importance ? All of these questions still remain unanswered today.

following page : Aerial view of Montségur.

The interior courtyard of Montségur castle.

Roquefixade Castle

Usson castle

ROQUEFIXADE

To the West of Lavelanet, Roquefixade castle stands in ruins on a steep cliff. From here, we have a view over St. Barthélémy, the Trois Seigneurs massif and Montségur peak. During the crusade against the Albigenses, the castle served as a Cathare refuge and was never captured by the crusaders.

USSON

The old walls of Usson, a large Cathare castle situated at the borders of the Ariège, Aude and Eastern Pyrénées regions now stand in ruins. Restored in the 17th and 18th centuries, it was dismantled during the Revolution. The last four fugitives from Montségur supposedly found refuge here with a part of the Cathare treasure.

PUIVERT

Near Quillan, on the road to Lavelanet,

Aerial view of Puivert castle

Puivert village is dominated by its castle built on a promontory. In 1210 after the surrender of Termes castle, it fell into the crusaders' hands after a battle of three days. A former summer residence of the Carcassonne viscounts, the castle stood above a lake at the time. The dyke broke open in 1279 and caused the devastation of the towns of Chalabre and Mirepoix. It was at Puivert in the 12th century that the great troubadours gathered around Ermengarde de Narbonne and Adelaïde de Carcassonne. Puivert was given to the Pons de Bruyères family after the crusade and was rebuilt in the early 14th century. It is characterised by its fortified door and its dungeon 35 metres high situated on an esplanade 80 metres long. Inside the dungeon, we can admire the chapel and the "musicians' room" which features sculptures of figures playing various instruments on the base of the vault ogives.

Fortified door of Puivert castle.

QUERIBUS

Quéribus on its rocky spur.

Above the picturesque village of Cucugnan, Quéribus fortress overlooks the entire Roussillon plain, the Albères, the Canigou and the Mediterranean. On this needle of rock and stone forming a powerful barrier is the castle, a solitary sentinel at 729 metres altitude, seemingly defying the elements. From Grau du Maury, a small path, then steps cut into the rock lead to the first walls which follow the relief of the mountain. After crossing the terraces, we reach the foot of the massive dungeon which is joined onto a 13th century square tower. The interior of the dungeon contrasts with the austere defensive aspect of the exterior. The main room is organised around a central cylindrical pillar. Eight ribs and four intersecting ribs lead outwards, supporting the vault. This Gothic room is completely unexpected in such a fortress and has raised many questions. As for Montségur, certain authors have put forward theories linked to the sun, comparing Quéribus dungeon to a "great solar calendar". Built in the 11th and 12th centuries, Quéribus castle was a large refuge for heretics during the crusade against the Albigenses. In 1255 and long after the surrender of Montségur, a military expedition was organised, led by the Seneschal of Carcassonne, Pierre d'Auteuil to take over the fortress commanded by the Cathare lord Chabert de Barbéra. Its surrender, together with that of Puilaurens, marked the last events of the Cathare epic in Languedoc. Transformed into a Royal fortress, Quéribus ensured the protection of the border between France and Aragon, then Spain until the Pyrénées treaty in 1659 when it lost its strategic importance.

Steps cut into the rock leading to the outer walls.

The fortifications.

The dungeon windows.

The pillar room.

PEYREPERTUSE

Aerial view of Peyrepertuse Castle.

After Caudiès de Fenouillèdes and Saint Paul de Fenouillet, you must cross the beautiful and impressive Galamus gorges to get to Peyrepertuse castle. Situated above the small village of Duilhac, this "aerial" fortress occupies an entire rocky rib 700 metres high. It is the finest example of Middle Age military architecture in Languedoc and behind its walls are dungeons, main-buildings, squares, churches and an interior castle.

There are two castles which must be distinguished from each other in the overall construction : the lower or 11th century Feudal castle which is the oldest and the upper or Royal castle, built in the second half of the 13th century. The lower castle features an old dungeon, Saint Mary church, the governor's residence and the water reservoir installed in the round tower. After the Western esplanade and the median wall, Saint Louis staircase cut into the rock leads to the Royal or Saint Jordi castle. It is built on the highest point and features a dungeon and chapel. From all sides of the rocky spur occupied by the castle, there is a splendid panorama of the entire region.

From Saint Jordi rock, view of the vestiges of the old castle.

PUILAURENS

After Quillan and after having crossed the narrow pass of Pierre Lys we must cross a small road to the left of Lapradelle village, to reach Puilaurens castle . Above Boulzane valley, the fortress stands on a spur whose rocks blend in with the walls forming an impressive defence body.

We reach the castle by way of a path, which once past the fortified door, leads to a vast courtyard 60 metres long, surrounded by high crenelated walls reinforced by two round towers. The dungeon and living quarters which constitute a second body are protected by other fortifications. This wall is equipped with two towers. Dame Blanche tower, situated to the south-west is the best conserved.

Puilaurens castle, possessed by the lords of Fenouillet, resisted the attacks of Simon de Montfort and the Royal army until the end of the crusade. Still sheltering a community of Cathares, the castle commanded by Chabert de Barbéra finally surrendered in 1255 or 1256. It was transformed into a Royal fortress and was attacked many times by the Spanish who captured it in 1636.

> **"THE FIVE SONS OF CARCASSONNE"**
> *The five Royal castles, Aguilar, Termes, Puilaurens, Quéribus and Peyrepertuse controlled by the protection of the border with Aragon, then Spain from the second half of the 13th century. During the Pyrénées treaty in 1659 which provided for the annexation of Roussillon to the French Crown, thus pushing back the border, these powerful fortresses in the South of the Kingdom soon lost their strategic importance.*

Puilaurens fortress.

Aerial view of Puilaurens Castle whose walls blend in with the rocky landscape.

The dungeon and living quarters protected by their wall.

Arques Castle.

ARQUES

Situated near Rialsesse forest, Arques castle is a square dungeon flanked by small corner towers inside its walls now in ruins. The dungeon with its two vaulted rooms one above the other can be visited. In the 13th and 14th centuries, the castle belonged to the de Voisins family who fought beside Simon de Montfort.

COUSTAUSSA

The impressive ruins of Coustaussa castle are situated opposite the small village of Rennes-le-Château which became famous for the enigma posed by its priest, Abbot Saunière and the treasure he supposedly found. Was is the Cathare treasure - or that of the Wisigoths ? Built by the family of the Viscounts of Trencavel, it was taken siege and occupied by Simon de Montfort's troops in 1211.

Coustaussa

Villerouge-Termenès

VILLEROUGE-TERMENES

Inside the village and overlooking the old houses, Villerouge-Termenès castle, owned by the Narbonne bishops, is characterised by its four massive corner towers. In 1321, the last known Cathare, Guillaume Bélibaste was burned in the castle courtyard.

TERMES

Only a few impressive ruins of this formidable castle, reputed as impregnable remain. For four months, it fiercely resisted

The ruins of Auriac Castle.

The ruins of Termes Castle.

the attacks of the crusaders' army. After the capture of Minerve in 1210, Raymond de Termes' citadel became the target of Simon de Montfort. "Situated at the summit of a very high mountain, surrounded by deep, inaccessible chasms, from which water flowed surrounding it on all sides", the castle seemed impregnable. The siege promised to be long and difficult. Initially, the castle was short of water and Raymond de Termes began the negotiations for its surrender. However providential rains changed the situation. Later, when the assailants reached the square one morning, they found it empty. Rats had polluted the water tanks and the garrison, suffering from dysentery, had evacuated the castle during the night.

The castle subsequently housed a Royal garrison, then much later became a hideout for the area's brigands before being dismantled in the 17th century.

AGUILAR

Situated near Tuchan, Aguilar castle stands on a rocky knoll above the Corbières vineyards. Taken by Simon de Montfort in 1210, it became part of the Royal domain in 1246. Its defence body is formed of a wall flanked by six round towers, built at the end of the 13th century on Royal order. Near the castle is the small Romanesque chapel dedicated to Saint Anne. The fortress which was one of the "five sons of Carcassonne" was abandoned at the end of the 16th century.

Durban-Corbières castle.

Padern castle, formerly possessed by the Abbot of La-grasse, overlooks the village.

Photographic credits
- Jean Mapas: pages 37 - 41
- J.D. Sudres: pages 30 - 38

GUIDES ALREADY PUBLISHED

IN THE  COLLECTION

Albi
Carcassonne
Luchon
Rocamadour
Toulouse-Lautrec Museum of Albi
Sainte-Cécile Basilica
Collioure
Ste-Enimie (Tarn Gorges)
Padirac chasm
Dargilan caves
Carennac
Lectoure
Notre Dame d'Orient
Sarlat and the Périgord Noir
Fürstenturm Andorra
St Cirq Lapopie
Gorges du Tarn
Pigeon-Houses of Midi Pyrénées
Tarn et Garonne
Habitations Caussenardes
Languedoc Roussillon
Auvergne

© 1996